HERMAN MELVILLE

HERMAN MELVILLE

THE TRAGIC VISION AND
THE HEROIC IDEAL

BY

STANLEY GEIST

1966

OCTAGON BOOKS, INC.

New York

Reprinted 1966
by special arrangement with Harvard University Press

OCTAGON BOOKS, INC.
175 FIFTH AVENUE
NEW YORK, N. Y. 10010

LIBRARY OF CONGRESS CATALOG CARD NUMBER: 66-18039

Printed in U.S.A. by
NOBLE OFFSET PRINTERS, INC.
NEW YORK 3, N. Y.

To

MY MOTHER AND FATHER

                    . . . but I saw
Too far into the sea; where every maw
The greater on the less feeds evermore: —
But I saw too distinct into the core
Of an eternal fierce destruction,
And so from happiness I far was gone.

                    — KEATS, Letter to Reynolds

        Good God, that men should desire
To search out that, which, being found
        kills all
The joy of life! — MARSTON, *The Malcontent*

HERMAN MELVILLE

THE TRAGIC VISION AND
THE HEROIC IDEAL

Heroism is the most persistent of romantic illusions. But to some men, among them Herman Melville, it is likewise the most necessary. A mere trick of the imagination, after all, makes a man write of King Lear rather than of the butcher's boy — an abnormality of vision by which the human animal bursts his shell of clay and assumes a more than earthly splendor. Melville's vision was in this respect more abnormal than that of most men, for his imagination was richer. Of all the demands which he made upon life, the most unremitting was the demand that it be heroic. The world of "bricks and shaven faces" [1] he found repulsive: he needed something more, and when he could not discover it in the visible facts he imposed it upon the facts or he created it. His most innocent self-dramatization betrayed a habit of imagining himself something other, something larger, than the Herman

(9)

Melville known to a few people in Albany and New York. Visiting his Berkshire neighbors, the Hawthornes, one evening, he narrated so graphically the prodigies of valor performed by a Pacific Island savage with a heavy club, that Mrs. Hawthorne asked, when he had gone, "Where is that club with which Mr. Melville was laying about him so?" [2] This is innocent enough, in truth; and yet there is a fundamental identity between the mature man who for a moment acted the part of a primitive warrior, and the boy who neglected his prayers in church to stare with awe at "the person who had been in Stony Arabia, and passed through strange adventures there." [3] The heroic ideal underwent more profound changes between his youth and his age than are apparent here; but in changing it did not become weaker: rather it was intensified.

Thus his mature considerations of democracy centered about the subject of heroism. It was his ardent wish that in democratic America, where the new continually corroded the old, where conventions of thought had not become frozen patterns, where no aristocracy of bastards' blood thwarted the rise of genuine merit, a new race of giants would arise, counterparts of the great giants who had walked abroad in former times. Often he believed that the new race had already sprung up: Kit Carson was his Hercules,[4] Andrew Jackson marched with Bunyan and Cervantes,[5] and the crew of a Yankee whaler were the descendants of those Gothic kings who stared silently from niches in old cathedrals. The proposition, "All men are created equal," inspired Melville only when it took the form, "All men are created equally capable of grandeur"; and it was to this second proposition alone that he penned his rhapsodic paean in *Moby Dick*:

If then, to meanest mariners, and renegades and castaways, I shall hereafter ascribe high qualities, though dark; weave round them tragic graces; if even the most mournful, perchance the most abased, among them all, shall at times lift himself to the exalted mounts; if I shall touch that workman's arm with some ethereal light; if I shall spread a rainbow over his disastrous set of sun; then against all mortal critics bear me out in it, thou just Spirit of Equality, which hast spread one royal mantle of humanity over all my kind! Bear me out in it, thou great democratic God! who didst not refuse to the swart convict Bunyan, the pale, poetic pearl; Thou who didst clothe with doubly hammered leaves of finest gold, the stumped and paupered arm of old Cervantes; Thou who didst pick up Andrew Jackson from the pebbles; who didst hurl him upon a war-horse; who didst thunder him higher than a throne! Thou who, in all Thy mighty, earthly marchings, ever cullest Thy selectest champions from the kingly commons; bear me out in it, O God![6]

The long chapter in *Moby Dick* on "The Honour and Glory of Whaling,"[7] and the two other chapters called "Knights and Squires,"[8] are significant; for Melville was never wholly realistic in *Moby Dick*: when he was most faithful to the facts, he was most careful to establish a relationship between those facts and a heroic ideal, medieval, mythological, or even Byzantine. It has been said that he dreamed of a brotherhood of men; but his dream was, in fact, of a brotherhood of supermen. "Believe me, my friends," he wrote in the essay on Hawthorne, "that men not very much inferior to Shakespeare are this day being born on the banks of the Ohio"; and in what followed he again betrayed the fervent hope beneath the confident affirmation:

This, too, I mean, that if Shakespeare has not been equalled, give the world time, and he is sure

to be surpassed in one hemisphere or the other.
Nor will it at all do to say that the world is getting
gray and grizzled now, and has lost that fresh
charm which she wore of old, and by virtue of
which the great poets of past times made themselves what we esteem them to be. Not so.
The world is as young today as when it was
created; and this Vermont morning dew is as wet
to my feet, as Eden's dew to Adam's.[9]

But if heroism in any form was one of the
deepest demands of his temperament, heroism in a single form came to bulk larger than
all others, and presided over the creation of
Moby Dick and *Pierre*. Such a development
was an almost inevitable adjunct to the
swift involution of his own mind, the swift
progression from the outwardness of *Typee*
and *Omoo* to the almost intolerable inwardness of *Pierre*, a work of painfully centrip-
etal nature, in which fact, episode, and
character are wholly subsumed in dominant
emotion and idea.[10] The record of Melville's creative life is a record of increasing
indifference to external things: his extensive
use of symbolism in *Pierre* was a virtual
proclamation that fact as fact, sensory experience as sensory experience, had ceased
to interest him for their own sake and had

become important only as the stuff through which he might express the nature of his greatest problem, the problem of Herman Melville. His works are the commentary upon his descent deeper and deeper into his own heart.

From my twenty-fifth year I date my life. Three weeks have scarcely passed, at any time between then and now, that I have not unfolded within myself.[11]

To unfold was to become aware of problems from which the self-blindness of his seafaring career had protected him; and at the moment when his outermost layer peeled away, Melville's life became a ceaseless, futile struggle to fathom the ambiguities of his own soul. He christened with the name of Fate [12] the irresistible power — either within or outside the sensitive individual — which drove him deeper and deeper into himself despite his most ardent desires to remain content with the sweet felicities of ignorance. And he had good reason both for using the metaphysical term to explain the personal problem, and for shrinking from the power which the term described. For the extreme inwardness of his self-scrutiny and the extreme outwardness of his scrutiny of the universe were in reality identical. To look into his own heart and to look into the heart of the cosmos were acts, for Melville, not only simultaneous but indistinguishable. Once his eyeballs had rolled the full turn inward, every new perception of the universe was a new perception of Herman Melville; and, conversely, every veil torn from the character of Herman Melville was a veil torn from the universe. In short, the universe came to reside within his own identity: his concept of Self expanded till it pressed against the walls of the cosmos. In his most earnest efforts to crystallize his thought, the perhaps unconscious fusion of World and Self in a single whole became most apparent:

Ten million things were as yet uncovered to Pierre. The old mummy lies buried in cloth on cloth; it takes time to unwrap this Egyptian king. Yet now, forsooth, because Pierre began to see through the first superficiality of the world, he fondly weens he has come to the unlayered substance. But, far as any geologist has yet gone down into the world, it is found to consist of nothing but surface stratified on surface. To its axis, the world being nothing but superinduced superficies. By vast pains we mine into the pyramid; by horrible gropings we come to the central room;

with joy we espy the sarcophagus; but we lift the lid — and no body is there! — appallingly vacant as vast is the soul of a man! [13]

Again, one of his favorite images or symbols was that which made use of contrasted sea and land, and he used this image interchangeably to represent either the world or the soul. On the one hand he sent Bulkington to sea on the *Pequod* with the words:

But as in landlessness alone resides the highest truth, shoreless, indefinite as God — so, better is it to perish in the howling infinite, than be ingloriously dashed upon the lee, even if that were safety! [14]

On the other hand, he wrote:

. . . consider them both, the sea and the land; and do you not find a strange analogy to something in yourself? For as this appalling ocean surrounds the verdant land, so in the soul of man lies one insular Tahiti, full of peace and joy, but encompassed by all the horrors of the half-known life. God keep thee! Push not off from that isle, thou canst never return! [15]

Self thus being synonymous with World, Melville's concept of the soul was dominated by the gigantic. The individual assumed an almost mythical magnitude in his thought. "The soul of a man" he could describe only by reference to what was most enormous in the physical world. The sarcophagus was not only appallingly vacant but appallingly vast. In one long and elaborate image in *Pierre* he drew upon both sea and mountains to express his concept of the soul, carrying his gigantism to its farthest limits:

But, as to the resolute traveller in Switzerland, the Alps do never in one wide and comprehensive sweep, instantaneously reveal their full awfulness of amplitude — their overawing extent of peak crowded on peak, and spur sloping on spur, and chain jammed behind chain, and all their wonderful battalionings of might; so hath heaven wisely ordained, that on first entering into the Switzerland of his soul, man shall not at once perceive its tremendous immensity; lest illy prepared for such an encounter, his spirit should sink and perish in the lowermost snows. Only by judicious degrees, appointed of God, does man come at last to gain his Mont Blanc and take an overtopping view of these Alps; and even then, the tithe is not shown; and far over the invisible Atlantic, the Rocky Mountains and the Andes are yet unbeheld. Appalling is the soul of a man! Better might one be pushed off into the material spaces beyond the uttermost orbit of our sun, than once feel himself fairly afloat in himself! [16]

By making the individual not only the focal point of his universe but also coextensive with it, Melville made the human drama not one of man upon a cosmic stage but of man upon the stage of himself. The individual was at once the actor, the play, and the playhouse. To Hawthorne he wrote:

There is a certain tragic phase of humanity which, in our opinion, was never more powerfully embodied than by Hawthorne. We mean the tragedies of human thought in its own unbiassed, native, and profounder workings.[17]

And in speaking of these "tragedies of human thought," these dramas contained wholly within the mind of the individual, Melville revealed more about himself than about Hawthorne.

2

He would have been a happier man, but not so important a man, if he had never invaded the pyramid to unwrap the mummy. For the pyramid was not only deep, it was dark also; and for every foot which he penetrated into the depths of life, he penetrated so far into its blackness. From a writer of travel books which spoke disrespectfully of missionaries, he became an explorer of tragedy, and the human situation became more intolerably tragic the longer he observed it. He knew nothing of "Evil" as a

own soul. To become aware of blackness one had first to become aware of oneself. Tragedy, in other words, lay not in the fact but in the individual's consciousness of the fact, and the more deep-thinking and sensitive the individual, the greater the tragedy. The clod did not feel the descending boot, and no man knew the frustration of the ideal by the actual whose sublunar intelligence had never groped beyond the visible fact to the desired possibility. Pierre and Ahab struggle with monsters which they have created within their own breasts. When Mrs. Glendinning and Mr. Falsgrave condemn Delly, the contrast set up between them and Pierre is not one of opposing moral standards, but of two modes of perception which have little to do with morality. Mrs. Glendinning and the Reverend reveal to Pierre that, in coming to a knowledge of mystery and of tragedy through Isabel, he has superseded a kind of vision previously acceptable. Thus the history of Pierre becomes the history of his struggle with his own apprehension of the world rather than with the world itself. His problem is not the objective fact that "Chronometricals" and "Horologicals," the way of Bacon and the way of Christ, are incompatible: most of the human race live on contentedly, indifferent to the opposition, accepting "a virtuous expediency" because largely untroubled by a dream of virtue stripped of expediency. The problem of Pierre is his too acute realization of the gulf between what is and what ought to be, between convention and truth. In recognizing the falsity of moral judgments accepted as valid because popular, of judgments upon human existence accepted as true because comfortable, he saddles himself with a vision of life at odds with the vision of other men, and the drama is that of his deeper but lonelier insight into the world. Not the thing itself, but the individual's awareness of the thing, was the province of Melville's art in *Moby Dick* and *Pierre*: not the ills that mere flesh was heir to, not disease or poverty or death, but the ills that mind, by its too keen vision, created of the gross stuff of experience. To suffer from the destruction of an ideal, one had first to create the ideal and then recognize its destruction.

So Ahab battles not with a thing and not with a principle, but with his own vision of

life which, in the form of the great White
Whale, has "gashed [his] body and torn
[his] soul."[19]

God help thee, old man, thy thoughts have
created a vulture in thee; and he whose intense
thinking thus makes him a Prometheus; a vulture
feeds upon his heart forever; that vulture the
very creature he creates.[20]

"Thy thoughts have created a vulture in
thee." For Ahab alone the White Whale is a
terrible incarnation: for the rest of the
Pequod's crew, Moby Dick is another whale
to be harpooned, slaughtered, and cooked
down to oil — with a gold doubloon reward
for the man who first sights him.

3

"I love all men who *dive*," he wrote to
E. A. Duyckinck.

Any fish can swim near the surface, but it takes
a great whale to go down stairs five miles or more;
and if he don't attain the bottom, why, all the
lead in Galena can't fashion the plummit that
will. I'm not talking of Mr. Emerson now, but
of the whole corps of thought-divers that have
been diving and coming up again with blood-shot
eyes since the world began.[21]

To dive, to plunge to the blackest depths of existence, he believed to be the noblest way of life. For those who did not dive he had little but scorn; and Shakespeare, who was the deepest diver of them all, sat enthroned among Melville's demigods.

By integrating this concept of heroism with his subjective notion of tragedy, Melville overstepped the bounds of a strictly democratic art: the capacity for profound self-scrutiny belonged to the spiritual nobleman alone, and not to Everyman. But only by becoming less democratic could he become more personal, and the one obsession of Melville the artist was the personality of Melville the man. If the crew of the *Pequod* are heroes, Ahab and Pierre are super-heroes by virtue of their deeper vision, and in Ahab and Pierre Melville most nearly portrayed himself. For he created them from the conviction that there was no true hero but a deep-diving hero, and that to be a deep diver was to be aware of the blackness at the heart of life. Thus the importance and the greatness of the tragic vision constituted a dominant theme of *Moby Dick* and *Pierre*. In diving deep, the superman fronted the terrors of the unseen world: Melville represented this motive in its simplest terms through the figure of Bulkington, who, just returned from a four years' voyage, was pushing off again without rest into the midwinter ocean:

Know ye now, Bulkington? Glimpses do ye seem to see of that mortally intolerable truth; that all deep, earnest thinking is but the intrepid effort of the soul to keep the open independence of her sea; while the wildest winds of heaven and earth conspire to cast her on the treacherous, slavish shore?

But as in landlessness alone resides the highest truth, shoreless, indefinite as God — so, better is it to perish in that howling infinite, than be ingloriously dashed upon the lee, even if that were safety! For worm-like, then, oh! who would craven crawl to land! Terrors of the terrible! is all this agony so vain? Take heart, take heart, O Bulkington! Bear thee grimly, demigod! Up from the spray of thy ocean-perishing — straight up, leaps thy apotheosis! [22]

And this passage is but the crystallization of a pattern of thought and imagery which recurs several times in *Moby Dick* and *Pierre.* There is, for example, the episode in which Melville draws an analogy between the Egyptian youth Memnon, Hamlet, and Pierre:

Now as the Memnon Statue survives down to this present day, so does that *nobly-striving* but ever *shipwrecked* character in some royal youths (for both Memnon and Hamlet were the sons of kings), of which that statue is the melancholy type; [23]

or the sentence in Pierre:

His *soul's ship* foresaw the inevitable rocks, but resolved to sail on, and make a *courageous wreck*.[24]

Melville's hero-worship was thus, in its deepest sense, not a worship of men but of a way of life which men sometimes attained. The distinguishing characteristic of this noblest way of life was depth — depth of thought, of emotion, of descent into oneself — and through this descent spiritual grandeur. But one could not make the descent and remain a happy man: to see profoundly was to see mournfully: life in its depths was not a thing of joy but of sorrow. Happiness, as Swift had discovered, was the condition of being well deceived, of supposing that the ocean yielded up all its secrets in the glistening of sunlight upon wave-crests. Far down, where the sun did not penetrate, five miles below the surface where only the great whales descended, was a profound blackness, an eternal fierce destruction which was the dark truth of life. The great whale came up with bloodshot eyes from these depths, and the great hero came up magnificent and sorrowful, far gone from the joys of those who saw only the sparkling of light on the waves. "Oh, now," cries Ahab, "Oh, now I feel my topmost greatness lies in my topmost grief." [25] That grief and greatness were inseparable was Melville's ripest conviction. Ahab becomes a demigod only after he is maddened with grief and hatred in his battle with Moby Dick. He arrives simultaneously at suffering and at grandeur. And Pierre, though originally a "royal-born" youth, becomes "divine," "superhuman," "Christlike," a "demigod," a "Titan," and "Prometheus" [26] by attaining the vision of tragedy and of mystery through Isabel.

The myth and the morality of the superman which Melville created differed in one significant detail from the comparable myths and moralities which have so often arisen in the modern world: they took no account of society. For, once again, the world of Melville was a subjective world, consisting not of things but of the individual's consciousness of things. And therefore the greatness of the Melville superman had nothing in common with the greatness of the Machiavellian or Marlovian superman: he rose to eminence not on the ruins of others but upon the ruins of his own less profound self. He did not conquer other men: he superseded himself. Greatness meant profundity and not power: the Czar was merely powerful, Leviathan was great. Indeed, Melville scorned the Tamburlaine variety of superman, who had power in the realm of men rather than greatness in the realm of his own soul:

For be a man's intellectual superiority what it will, it can never assume the practical, available supremacy over other men, without the aid of some sort of external arts and intrenchments, always, in themselves, more or less paltry and base. That it is, that forever keeps God's true princes of the Empire from the world's hustings; and leaves the highest honours that this air can give, to those men who become famous more through their inferiority to the choice hidden handful of the Divine Inert, than through their undoubted superiority over the dead level of the mass.[27]

Greatness, in other words, through conquest over one's own surface-skimming self, was a fundamental concept in Melville's art. "Nor will the tragic dramatist who would depict mortal indomitableness in its fullest sweep and direct swing, ever forget a hint . . . so important." [28]   And if these notions were aristocratic in their indifference to the society of men, in their independence of mass appraisal, and in their assumption of ultimate gradations in spiritual nobility, they were democratic also in ignoring degrees of temporal rank and wealth, and in allowing to the most humble man the privilege (if not always the ability) of acting the hero in his own theater:

But Ahab, my captain, still moves before me in all his Nantucket grimness and shagginess; and in this episode touching emperors and kings, I must not conceal that I have only to do with a poor old whale-hunter like him; and, therefore, all outward majestical trappings and housings are denied me. Oh, Ahab! what shall be grand in thee, it must needs be plucked at from the skies, and dived for in the deep, and featured in the unbodied air! [29]

Since the individual contained his own world within himself, acting there and achieving greatness in the eyes of himself alone, snatching it from the skies, the deep, and the unbodied air, Melville believed that

(28)

his theoretic democracy and his aloofness
from other men were not incompatible:

> It seems an inconsistency to assert uncondi-
> tional democracy in all things, and yet confess a
> dislike to all mankind — in the mass. But not
> so.[30]

"But not so": for democracy in his thought
had nothing to do with the relationship of
man to man, being simply the equal privilege
of all men to achieve heroism within themselves. By stripping from his concept of
heroism all canons but that of isolated spiritual stature, Melville could be democratic
without being sociable: the poorest Nantucket whaling captain might soar high
above the Czar, but was in no way con-
nected with the existence of the Czar.

In other words, his was a democracy of
man thinking and of man feeling, not of man
acting, and it ignored the social and political
relationships of living human beings. It
was a democracy of the men of all ages and
nations in a world of disembodied thought
and feeling, where one might be closer to
Solomon than to one's neighbor. Proclaiming, on the one hand, liberty, equality, and
fraternity in a universe of spirit, Melville

ignored, on the other hand, the universe of flesh and blood and political parties. He could be a complete democrat in one world, embracing in a brotherhood of spirit royal Hamlet and humble Cervantes; yet contemn and remain aloof from the society about him. The creative mind in quest of affinities is indifferent to bounds of space and time, discarding at its moment of greatest intensity all rubrics but that of ultimate kinship of sensibility; and it was in respect to such kinship that Melville was most profoundly democratic. The political or theoretic problem of society and the individual as understood by his contemporaries thus had for him slight meaning: he transcended it by disregarding society altogether, and by placing the entire sphere of action within the consciousness of the individual. To be sure, he could not so easily annihilate the problem in its emotional rather than its theoretic aspects — that is, when it ceased to be Individual versus Society and became Loneliness versus Brotherhood. But this is another question, to be considered later.

4

By descending into the depths of himself and attaining the tragic vision, man became sorrowful and he acquired a heart. For by "heart" Melville meant the richness of spirit which could be gained in this way only. The opposition which he set up between Heart and Head was not simply an opposition of emotion to intellect. He knew himself too well to be comfortable before any such cleavage of man into well defined categories of thought and feeling as Hawthorne proposed in *Ethan Brand* or in *The House of Seven Gables*. In a letter to Hawthorne on *Ethan Brand*, one discerns Melville's discomfort, imperfectly expressed but unmistakable:

It is a frightful poetical creed that the cultivation of the brain eats out the heart. But it's my *prose* opinion that in most cases, in those men who have fine brains and work them well, the heart extends down to hams. And though you smoke them with the fire of tribulation, the head only gives the richer and the better flavor.[31]

Analytic thought was heartless, to be sure; but emotion without thought was mere sentiment. Thus, in Melville's unstated terms, the conversion of Hawthorne's Hollingsworth from a life of cold, rational analysis to a life of vapid and unreasoning marital bliss with Phoebe, was a conversion from the head but not to the heart. For heart implied concentration and not expansion, intensity and not ease. And intensity of being could be attained only if the entire man was brought into focus — his powers of thought as well as his powers of feeling. The great mind was integral to the great heart, not opposed to it. One could not comprehend the blackness of life by any extension of feeling, but only by a concentration of both thought and feeling. And until one had comprehended that blackness, one was no more than a sentimentalizer in truth, a Phoebe, a sighing, misty-eyed creature paddling about in a cockle-shell on a blue lagoon. Bacon was a rationalizer, but Christ had a heart: which is to say, Christ possessed that richness of spirit which could be gained only through the knowledge of sorrow, while Bacon had a mere analyzing brain, like that of a watchmaker.

"We begin to live when we have conceived life as tragedy," wrote Yeats:[32] the discovery meant for Yeats the difference between "Oisin" and "Sailing to Byzantium"; for Melville, the difference between *Typee* and *Moby Dick*. Melville left a detailed record of the discovery itself in *Pierre* — a record obscured by a narrative method which whirls dizzily from the grotesquely bad to the grotesquely good — that deserves the closest examination for what it reveals of the author.

Pierre is walking by the river at night. He stops by a giant pine tree which towers into the darkness overhead, sits down at its base, and observes a great root extending to the river bank. As he studies it, the tree becomes for him a symbol of mingled nobility and sorrow:

How wide, how strong these roots must spread! Sure this pine-tree takes powerful hold of this fair earth! Yon bright flower hath not so deep a root. This tree hath outlived a century of that gay flower's generations, and will outlive a century of them yet to come. This is most sad. . . . Oh, tree! so mighty thou, so lofty, yet so mournful! This is most strange! [33]

As he looks up into the branches, there suddenly appears to him the face of the girl he is to know as Isabel. He is troubled, yet cannot understand the full significance of his vision: the dark, sorrowful face demands an emotion which he has not experienced:

Yet I have never known thee, Grief; thou art a legend to me. . . . I know thee not, — do half disbelieve in thee.[34]

But the face presses upon him more strongly. Premonitions and vague fears seize him.

If thou hast a secret in thy eyes of mournful mystery, out with it. . . . Now, never into the soul of Pierre, stole there before a muffledness like this! . . . I conjure ye to lift the veil.[35]

The face vanishes, leaving him less tense but still somewhat fearful. He thinks of Lucy, of the volumes which they will thumb together — Flaxman's Homer, and his Dante — but no, not Dante:

Night's and Hell's poet he. No, we will not open Dante. Methinks now the face — the face — minds me a little of pensive, sweet Francesca's face — or, rather, as it had been Francesca's daughter's face — wafted on the sad dark wind, toward observant Virgil and the blistered Florentine. No, we will not open Flaxman's Dante.[36]

Soon afterwards, he sees Isabel herself. There is a crucial moment of recognition, and then, at home, Pierre realizes that he has undergone a change as a result of a new insight: beneath the superficial world of the senses in which he has lived till now, there lurks a world of mystery, of wonder interlocked with wonder, the perception of which is in fact the perception of his own soul:

. . . we ourselves are greater miracles, and superber trophies than all the stars in universal space. . . . Explain thou this strange integral feeling in me myself, he thought — turning upon the fancied face — and I will then renounce all other wonders, to gaze wonderingly at thee. But thou hast evoked in me profounder spells than the evoking one, thou face! For me thou hast uncovered one infinite, dumb, beseeching countenance of mystery, underlying all the surfaces of visible time and space.[37]

The knowledge of Isabel is thus the knowledge of mystery. And Melville once more emphasizes the fact that this mystery resides in the universe conceived not as a thing apart from Pierre, but as a thing within him:

From without, no wonderful effect is wrought within ourselves, unless some interior, responding wonder meets it. . . . No cause have we to fancy, that a horse, a dog, a fowl, ever stand transfixed beneath yon skyey load of majesty. But our soul's arches underfit into its; and so prevent the upper arch from falling on us with unsustainable inscrutableness. "Explain ye my deeper mystery," said the shepherd Chaldean king, smiting his breast, lying on his back upon the plain; "and then, I will bestow all my wonderings upon ye, ye stately stars!" [38]

The knowledge of Isabel takes on even further significance: the arrival of her letter precipitates psychological chaos. But Pierre refuses to retreat. "Henceforth I will know nothing but Truth." [39] And in a torrential outburst of language he proclaims his intent:

Oh! falsely guided in the days of my Joy am I now truly led in this night of my grief? — I will be a raver, and none shall stay me! I will lift my hand in fury, for am I not struck? I will be bitter in my breath, for is not this cup of gall? Thou Black Knight, that with visor down, thus confrontest me, and mockest at me; lo! I strike through thy helm, and will see thy face, be it Gorgon! . . . From all idols I tear all veils; henceforth I will see the hidden things; and live right out in my own hidden life! [40]

Pierre's entire moral universe is overturned. The cherished image of his father, symbol of the supposed purity of the world, is destroyed when Isabel reveals that Mr. Glendinning was her father also. And yet there is some compensation:

. . . the heavier woes . . . both purge the soul of gay-hearted errors and replenish it with a saddened truth.[41]

He is granted a sudden insight into the character of his mother:

She well might have stood all ordinary tests; but when Pierre thought of the touchstone of his immense strait applied to her spirit; he felt profoundly assured that she would crumble into nothing before it.[42]

Now her great limitation, which is the limitation of the world she represents, becomes clear: she is *heartless*, for she lacks the vision of tragedy and of mystery:

Oh heartless, proud, ice-gilded world, how I hate thee, he thought, that thy tyrannous, insatiate grasp, thus now in my bitterest need — thus doth rob me even of my mother.[43]

Her pride, her ease, her serenity derive from a failure ever to have penetrated to those darker depths of which Pierre has just become conscious. She is proud because blind, comfortable because heartless. She is of the conventional world, which survives in confidence, dullness, and contentment by suppressing that part of itself which would, in penetrating to the truth, in revealing life to be essentially tragic, simultaneously give sorrow and fullness to existence. Pierre, discovering the somber richness of which human life at its supreme moments is capable, discovers also "the dreary heart-vacancies of the conventional life." [44] Since his mother belongs to that conventional life, and he now to another, their relationship becomes impossible. The way of convention is the way of cowardice, of evasion, of failure to look into the heart of darkness. To know truth is to know sorrow also, and to leave behind the joys which spring from less profound vision. But only through such sorrow and through such profound vision does a man achieve true greatness, true heart-fullness:

Oh, now I know the night, and comprehend the sorceries of the moon, and all the dark persuadings that have their birth in storm and winds. Oh, not long will Joy abide, when Truth doth come; nor Grief her laggard be. Well may this head hang on my breast, — it holds too much; well may my heart knock at my ribs, — prisoner impatient of his iron bars. Oh, men are jailors all; jailors of themselves; and in Opinion's world ignorantly hold their noblest part a captive to their vilest; as disguised royal Charles when caught by peasants. The heart! the heart! 'tis God's anointed; let me pursue the heart! [45]

Thus the triumph of the heart is not a triumph over the head but over heartlessness; it is not a victory of emotion over mind, but a focussing of thought and feeling for an intuitive perception into the tragedy of existence. When this is recognized, the meaning of Melville's opposition of Heart and Head becomes more clear. It was the opposition, so to speak, of poetry to physics, of intuitive perception for the sake of life to analytic perception for the sake of science. Or, better, Head implied abstract speculation, while Heart meant "comprehension of the mystery of life." [46] But one must not be led, by the inadequate nature of the terminology, to suppose that the opposition of Heart to Head was merely that of careless and wishful thinking to precise thinking. The testimony of experience outweighs the limitations of the critical jargon, and if the terms are exasperating, the reality is unmistakable. "I have never yet been able to perceive how anything can be known for truth by consecutive reasoning," [47] wrote Keats, and Middleton Murry's comment upon Keats' statement illuminates admirably the entire matter:

. . . rational thought is based, not one whit less than poetic thought, upon an assumption which is also for the most part unconscious. Rational thought *assumes* that reality is rational. Once we have seen that this is an assumption, we shall also see the futility of criticizing poetic thought because it is irrational. One might as well criticize rational thought for being unpoetic. What we have to understand and to accept is the fact that there are two orders or kinds of thinking, and that the only means of deciding which of them brings us nearer to reality is by the completeness of the ultimate satisfaction which they bring. There is absolutely no objective criterion by which one can be preferred to the other.[48]

If one carry this a step further, still more difficulties which appear in Melville's work resolve themselves. One may consider, for example, the subject of "Melville and the philosophers." He expressed, in *Moby Dick*, an unformulated dissatisfaction with philosophers in general. He spoke contemptuously of "Plato's honey head." [49] Half in earnest, half in jest, he compared the heads of a right whale and a sperm whale hoisted on opposite sides of the *Pequod* to Kant and Locke, suggesting, "Oh, ye foolish! throw all these thunderheads overboard, and then you will float light and right." [50] Later he compared the same two whales to a Stoic and "a Platonian, who might have taken up Spinoza in his later years." [51] These are hardly serious outbursts, and yet they are significant in the light of developments in *Pierre*. For in this book Melville's dissatisfaction became bitter revulsion:

Certain philosophers have time and again pretended to have found the secret of life; but if they do not in the end discover their own delusion, other people soon discover it for themselves, and so those philosophers and their vain philosophy are let glide away into practical oblivion. Plato, and Spinoza, and Goethe, and many more belong to this guild of self-imposters, with a preposterous rabble of Muggletonian Scots and Yankees, whose vile brogue still the more bestreaks the stripedness of their Greek or German Neoplatonic originals. [52]

He jested at the expense of Hobbes, Berkeley, Descartes, and Kant, [53] though allowing them a certain fundamental greatness for their speculative efforts. But the bitterest outcry of all he made Pierre put in the mouth of his author-hero:

A deep-down, unutterable mournfulness is in me. Now I drop all humorous or indifferent disguises, and all philosophic pretensions. . . . Hopelessness and despair are over me, as pall on pall. Away, ye chattering apes of a sophomorean Spinoza and Plato, who once didst all but delude

me that night was day, and pain only a tickle.
Explain this darkness, exorcise this devil, ye
cannot.[54]

The philosophers — all of them, and not
simply one or another — were infuriating
and absurd not because their systems were
opposed to his, but because their thought
was systematized, hence heartless:

Corporations have no souls, and thy Pantheism,
what was that? Thou wert but the pretentious,
heartless part of a man. Lo! I hold thee in this
hand, and thou art crushed in it like an egg from
which the meat hath been sucked.[55]

All philosophic unity was both analytic and
eclectic; while any unity which was to be
valid for Melville had to be intuitive and
inclusive — in other words, perceived by the
great heart, not by the watchmaker's brain;
and the great heart was that which was filled
with the vision of tragedy. "Faith and
philosophy are air," he wrote, "but events
are brass." [56] The philosophers had con-
structed their universe of shapes of air, not
having felt the touch of brass. They were
pretentious without stature, for stature
meant that mournful richness of soul which
came only through a knowledge of the dark-

ness of life. Men began to live when they conceived life as tragedy. The philosophers, by attempting to evade or to explain away tragedy, revealed that they were dead things, "like an egg from which the meat hath been sucked." The world of Mrs. Glendinning and the world of Kant and Goethe and Spinoza, were therefore alike in their want of a heart. Both pretended to exist without "the ocean, which is the dark side of the earth, and which is two-thirds of this earth." [57] Neither, as a result, could be heroic; and neither had anything to say to Melville.

It is obvious, then, that any interpretation of *Moby Dick* which represents the book as a metaphysical drama, or as a systematized scheme in which every character and every incident is carefully integrated in a pattern of thought, becomes absurd. Such a mode of apprehending life or of presenting life was repulsive to Melville: any attempt to reduce life to a set of abstractions, or to impose an ordered system upon an irrational universe, was both presumptuous and heartless. He recognized, deeply if not clearly, that between the metaphysical mind and his own was the same split which has always

separated the philosopher from the creative artist: all his thought constituted a
mode of perception, all the thought of the
philosopher constituted a reasoned scheme.
And though philosophy was but the ration-
alization of vision, the philosopher yet distinguished himself from the creative artist
by being concerned with vision as system
while the artist was concerned with vision
as life. If there was an eternal war of
metaphysical Good with metaphysical Evil
in the mad gyrations of the spheres, Melville
knew nothing about it. But he was obsessed
with the eternal drama which he saw within
the profoundest men, and within them only:
the drama whose Chorus endlessly intoned,
"We begin to live when we have conceived
life as tragedy."

5

Grief and Greatness, suffering and heroism: these were, to Melville, inseparable;
and they were the theme of his two most
ambitious books. Nowhere does *Moby Dick*
more nearly become one with the work
which inspired it, *King Lear*,[58] than in its
penetration by this double theme. And

nowhere, interestingly enough, does it more nearly approximate the very letter of *King Lear* than in the imagery through which the motive of heroic suffering is expressed. As in *Lear*, the sense of mental suffering is maintained by

the general floating image, kept constantly before us, chiefly by means of the verbs used, but also in metaphor, of a human body in anguished movement, tugged, wrenched, beaten, pierced, stung, scourged, dislocated, flayed, gashed, scalded, tortured, and finally broken on the rack.[59]

With the first appearance of Ahab on deck the note is struck:

He looked like a man cut away from the stake when the fire has overrunningly wasted all the limbs without consuming them. . . .[60]

And from that point the image recurs, like a musical phrase with variations, in virtually every scene in which Ahab is mentioned. Tortured by his *blazing brain*,[61] at night,

with glaring eyes Ahab would burst from his stateroom as though escaping from a bed that was on fire.[62]

Starbuck reads in Ahab's eyes " some lurid woe that would *shrivel* me up; "[63] and

Ishmael speaks of " that *burnt-out* crater of his brain." [64] Ahab is driven on in his pursuit of Moby Dick by

all that most *maddens* and *torments* . . . all that *cracks the sinews and cakes the brain.*[65]

The *jagged* edge of his iron crown of woe *galls* [66] him as he proceeds in his *brain-battering* fight.[67]

He piled upon the whale's white hump the sum of all the general rage and hate felt by his whole race from Adam down; and then, as if his chest had been a mortar, he *burst his hot heart's shell* upon it.[68]

His *torn* body and *gashed* soul *bleed* into one another.[69] He is

gnawed within and *scorched* without, with the unrelenting *fangs* of some incurable idea.[70]

He stands before his men "with a *crucifixion* in his face." [71]

"God! God! God! — *crack* my heart! *stave* my brain!" [72] he cries in despair. His passion, *like a hawk's beak, pecks* [73] his brain. He is *shrivelled* [74] by his woe.

The lightning flashes through my skull; mine eyeballs *ache* and *ache*; my whole *beaten* brain seems as *beheaded* and rolling on some *stunning* ground.[75]

A *vulture feeds* upon his heart.[76] He is like the

lofty trunk of a great tree, when the upper lightning *tearingly darts* down it . . . leaving the tree
still alive, but *branded*.[77]

But through his suffering Ahab is en-
nobled. Melville wrote in *Pierre*, "Not to
know Gloom and Grief is not to know aught
that an heroic man should learn." [78] And he
made it plain in both *Moby Dick* and *Pierre*
that suffering and heroism were concomitant.
Ahab soliloquizes at sunset:

Is then the crown too heavy that I wear? This
Iron Crown of Lombardy [which was made of the
nails used in the Crucifixion].

And he continues:

Yet is it bright with many a gem; I, the wearer,
see not its far flashings; but darkly feel that I
wear that, that dazzlingly confounds.[79]

Melville would leave no doubts of Ahab's
magnificence. The crown of woe, with its
jagged, galling edges, shines "bright with
many a gem," its brilliance dazzling and
confounding. And Ahab, like Pierre, is
exalted far above all common mortals. He
is "a lone gigantic elm," a Norse king. He

is Prometheus, and he is Adam, "staggering beneath the piled centuries since Paradise."[80]

Melville's firm conviction that man became a hero of gigantic stature by attaining the vision of tragedy, and his equally firm conviction that he was himself among the giants, made his use of the Prometheus symbol particularly appropriate. For if the greatness of the individual, residing wholly within his own vision of the world, was contingent upon no one and nothing outside himself, what distinction remained on the timeless and bodiless spiritual plane between human and superhuman? "To trail the genealogies of these high mortal miseries," he wrote in *Moby Dick*, " carries us at last among the sourceless primogenitures of the gods." [81] What more could the gods themselves know of the depths of the human tragedy than the profoundest men? If no more, why should the hero abase himself before any powers, human or superhuman? He compared Hawthorne (and so himself, for his comments on Hawthorne are habitually self-portraits) [82] to

the man who . . . declares himself a sovereign nature (in himself) amid the powers of heaven, hell, and earth. He may perish; but so long as he exists he insists upon treating with all Powers upon an equal basis. If any of those other Powers choose to withhold certain secrets, let them; that does not impair my sovereignty in myself; that does not make me tributary.[83]

And in another letter to Hawthorne he remarked:

You perceive I employ a capital initial in the pronoun referring to the Deity; don't you think there is a slight dash of flunkeyism in that usage? [84]

So Promethean defiance of the gods and intense pride, were other elements in the nature of the tragic hero. Pierre and Ahab habitually defy all the powers of all the spheres, and the pride of each is immense. But their pride, and Melville's, springs not out of conceit or vanity but out of suffering; and it must be carefully distinguished from that false pride in external beauty and material wealth which Pierre finds so revolting in his mother. It has in it, to be sure, something of the self-reliant spirit, but is, at bottom, a corollary to the belief that man becomes god-like in attaining the tragic vision. None but the mighty could look into the heart of darkness, and it was sheer hypocrisy to pretend ignorance of one's own might. If the sense of sorrowful greatness which accompanied the tragic vision was illusory, it was yet a clear intuition, rather than a wishful thought imposed upon experience: there was no mistaking the fact of sorrow, and no mistaking the instinctive supposition that sorrow was a nobler emotion than joy.

For, thought Ahab, even the highest earthly felicities ever have a certain unsignifying pettiness lurking in them, but, at bottom, all heart-woes a mystic significance, and, in some men, an archangelic grandeur. . . . The ineffaceable, sad birth-mark in the brow of a man is but the stamp of sorrow in the signers.[85]

Ahab, in his Promethean greatness, is thus "proud as a Greek god." [86] Soliloquizing upon the "dark Hindu half of nature" — all the blackness which he feels in the world — he cries out:

Yet dost thou, darker half, rock me with a prouder, if a darker faith.[87]

In proclaiming his sovereign power, the hero also proclaimed his solitude. Ahab, studying the figures stamped upon his doubloon, sees his own nature mirrored in them and says:

There's something ever egotistical in mountain-tops and towers and all other grand and lofty things; look here, — three peaks as proud as Lucifer. The firm tower, that is Ahab; the volcano, that is Ahab; the courageous, the un-daunted and victorious fowl, that too is Ahab.[88]

"As proud as Lucifer" — a conventional simile, to be sure; but Melville, like his hero, admired the rebel archangel for his proud and heroic defiance. He wrote of the tail of the Leviathan:

Out of the bottomless profundities the gigantic tail seems spasmodically snatching at highest heaven. So in dreams have I seen majestic Satan thrusting forth his tormented colossal claw from the flame Baltic of Hell.[89]

With this, at least one difficulty of *Pierre* resolves itself. Melville's attempt to deal simultaneously with the theme most pro-foundly his own, that of tragic heroism, and the theme which was his for but a short time while under the influence of Carlyle, that of self-renunciation in the "Enthusiast to Duty," [90] was doomed to failure. Tragic heroism meant pride and assertion of self;

enthusiasm to Duty meant humility and submission of self. He had already, in *Moby Dick*, contrasted the noble strength of God the Father as painted by Michelangelo with the epicene weakness of Christ the Son as painted in those "soft, curled, hermaphroditical Italian pictures in which his idea has been most successfully embodied":

. . . these pictures, so destitute as they are of all brawniness, hint nothing of any power, but the mere negative, feminine one of submission and endurance, which on all hands it is conceded, form the peculiar practical virtues of his teachings.[91]

The reconciliation of a pagan concept of heroic suffering with a Christian concept of humble suffering was impossible. And Melville's attempt at such a reconciliation in *Pierre* resulted only in the baffling alternate fusion and splitting of the Prometheus-image and the Christ-image. Sincerely as he might try, he was temperamentally unable to accept Christ until he had made him a Promethean hero. The motive of spiritual Titanism is even more predominant in *Pierre* than in *Moby Dick*. It appears not only in images which recur again and again,

but in such broader aspects of the book as the underlying Hamlet-analogy, the legend of the Memnon Stone,[92] and the vision of Enceladus' battle with the Mount of the Titans.[93] Pierre himself has a "Titanic soul," [94] and he bears up "like a demi-god."[95] At his moment of bitterest frustration,

. . . he began to feel in him that the thews of a Titan were forestallingly cut by the scissors of Fate.[96]

When he professes to be most Christ-like, he is in fact most like Prometheus.

6

Pierre ends in disaster, as it must. But before it ends the hero himself gives the key to the drama:

. . . the fool of Truth, the fool of Virtue, the fool of Fate, now quits ye forever! [97]

It is clear enough to anyone familiar with *Pierre* why he is the fool of Virtue; and clear enough for the present purpose why he is the fool of Fate. But the meaning of "Truth" is not so obvious. Pierre uses the word in a similar fashion more than once before: the most important occasion is when he discovers Isabel, sees for the first time into the depths, turns in bitter fury upon "the dreary heart-vacancies of the conventional life," and cries, "The heart! the heart! 'tis God's annointed; let me pursue the heart!"[98] On that occasion, renouncing his mother, renouncing the prosperity and external beauty of their lives which have kept him from the vision of darkness, Pierre says:

Oh, small thanks I owe thee, Favourable Goddess, that didst clothe this form with all the beauty of a man, that so thou mightest hide from me all the truth of a man. Now I see that in his beauty a man is snared, and made stone-blind, as the worm within its silk. Welcome then be Ugliness and Poverty and Infamy and all ye other crafty ministers of Truth, that beneath the hoods and rags of beggars hide yet the belts and crowns of kings.[99]

The Truth of a man was that Christ-like mournfulness and Promethean grandeur of which he was capable at his greatest moments: that part of himself which was held captive by the world of Convention and Opinion:

Oh, men are jailors all; jailors of themselves; and in Opinion's world ignorantly hold their noblest

part a captive to their vilest; as disguised royal Charles when caught by peasants.[100]

The discovery of Isabel is, for Pierre, the discovery of that spiritual depth in human life which lies deep hidden under a surface of convention, of ostentation, and of outward ornament; and the acceptance of Isabel is the acceptance of that revelation of Truth. Truth means sorrow, indeed:

Oh, not long will Joy abide when Truth doth come; nor Grief her laggard be. Well may this head hang on my breast, — it holds too much; well may my heart knock at my ribs, — prisoner impatient of his iron bars.

But Truth is the heart of a man: without it he is but a hollow shell. Therefore —

The heart! the heart! 'tis God's annointed; let me pursue the heart! [101]

From this episode to the end, *Pierre* is a study of the pursuit of the heart and of its consequences: apotheosis, solitude, and destruction. For in ennobling himself man destroys himself. Just as the inheritors of the earth are the heartless Mrs. Glendinnings and the Bacons with their watchmakers' brains; just as the Christian ethic is impossible where "a virtuous expediency" is the highest that can be expected; so in a world of mere mortals there is no place for the demigod: he is doomed to smash his hot heart's shell upon the power within himself which has exalted him above other men without stripping him of every taint of humanity. The god-like fire is enclosed in a shell of clay. God enough to attain the vision of darkness, he remains human enough so that his vision becomes unbearable. In the end he destroys himself upon his own knowledge of the Truth.

Bulkington, who wins apotheosis by his courageous fronting of the dark ocean, is also destroyed, for his, too, is a "mortally intolerable truth." [102] "Look not into the heart of the fire, O man. . . ." [103] "There is a wisdom that is woe, but there is a woe that is madness. . . ." [104]

Hence the incest symbol in *Pierre*: in its most basic terms, incest is the symbol of introversion. In turning from the life of externality represented in Lucy to the knowledge of life's dark subsurface represented by Isabel, Pierre turns inward upon himself, and embraces the deeper part of his own

identity. In the end, his action ennobles him and destroys him:

. . . her whole form sloped sideways, and she fell upon Pierre's heart, and her long hair ran over him, and arboured him in ebon vines.[105]

Hence, too, the dream of the incestuous Titan storming the mountains in an attempt to regain his paternal birthright of complete godliness, but forever held down by his terrestrial mother's legacy of clay. And hence, finally, Ahab wreaking his bitterness and hatred upon the White Whale, who is for him, and for him alone, that vision of darkness which is the monstrous cause of his suffering and of his magnificence:

The White Whale swam before him as the monomaniac incarnation of those malicious agencies which some deep men feel eating in them. . . .[106]

Ahab's god-like pride is fatal. But it is also magnificent. And the logical conclusion that magnificence is fatal is a basic theme in *Moby Dick* and *Pierre*. The hero is destroyed. But the important thing is that he is heroic. Ahab's thoughts have created a vulture in his own breast — but his "intense thinking thus makes him a Prometheus." [107]

And *Pierre*, though frenzied with self-revulsion, yet sees his own head upon the armless trunk of the giant Enceladus:

For it is according to eternal fitness, that the precipitated Titan should still seek to regain his paternal birthright even by fierce escalade. Wherefore whoso storms the sky gives best proof he came from thither! But whatso crawls contented in the moat before that crystal fort, shows it was born within that slime, and there forever will abide.[108]

And the Titan was doomed not only to ultimate destruction but to loneliness in life as well. "Oh, lonely death on lonely life!" cries Ahab, "Now do I feel my topmost greatness lies in my topmost grief!" [109] By his solitary descent into the depths of life, man became a demigod. But the earth was a place of men, and the act of becoming a demigod was therefore the act of isolating oneself from men while yet remaining incapable of complete godhead. It was a magnificent isolation, to be sure, like that of a giant mountain peak rising out of the sea, but yet isolation; all the spontaneous communal joys of simpler men left far below one's reach in the attainment of one's gigantic stature. Other men walked blind and undisturbed in

their world of "bricks and shaven faces," but the temples of heaven were golden, and mighty Jove was bearded, and Herman Melville was doomed forever to compare the lesser with the greater, finding one impossible, the other intolerable. He must pay a terrible price for his giant's stature. If he walked above the crowd he could not be of it — but neither, on the other hand, could he escape from it:

Then he staggered back upon himself, and only found support in himself. Then Pierre felt that deep in him lurked a divine unidentifiableness, that owned no earthly kith or kin. Yet was this feeling entirely lonesome and orphan-like. Fain, then, for one moment would he have recalled the thousand sweet illusions of Life; though purchased at the price of Life's Truth; so that once more he might not feel himself driven out an infant Ishmael into the desert, with no maternal Hagar to accompany and comfort him.[110]

Pierre and Ahab are supermen, but they are not inhuman, so they are isolated from men and from the gods:

Ahab stands alone among all the millions of the peopled earth, nor gods nor men his neighbors! [111]

Pierre . . . in his deepest, highest part, was utterly without sympathy, divine, human, brute, or vegetable.[112]

And the entire responsibility — for apotheosis, for destruction, for solitude — lay upon that irresistible instinct which turned some men in upon themselves and forced upon them the knowledge of the world in their own souls. "Oh, life! 'tis in an hour like this, with soul beat down and held to knowledge, — as wild, untutored things are forced to feed — Oh, life! 'tis now that I do feel the latent horror in thee." [113]

Self and World were identical. Ahab, standing before his doubloon, soliloquizes:

. . . this round gold is but the image of the rounder globe, which, like a magician's glass, to each and every man in turn but mirrors back his own mysterious self.[114]

And as Starbuck and Stubb and King-Post and the Manxman and Queequeg and Fedaliah and Pip in turn study the doubloon, each sees reflected in it his own knowledge, beliefs, desires, and aspirations. But Ahab alone is aware that every man sees a different world: Ahab alone knows the meaning of isolation.

For if the world mirrored back to every man not one reality for all, but to each man his own mysterious self, then not only did

every man contain his own world, but each
world was distinct from every other. The
universe ceased to be an organized whole;
unity became chaos and anarchy; and human
existence was governed by but one principle: isolation. And yet, isolation itself was
a meaningless term so long as it remained a
principle: if men lived not in the reality but
in their consciousness of the reality, then no
man was truly isolated until he became aware
of his isolation. A thousand widely shared
conventions and traditions and emotions
served to buttress mankind's great illusion of
brotherhood, to conceal from all but a chosen
few the dark knowledge that every man was
eternally entombed within the marble walls
of his own identity. By looking deep into his
own heart, the individual discovered simultaneously the darkness and the loneliness of
his life. To discover isolation was to become
isolated, and the chosen few who made the
discovery thereby cut themselves off from
men and gods. But by the same token —
and here was the paradox — these few also
established a subtle, impalpable bond of
solidarity among themselves, which transcended their isolation without relieving it:

tional experience is opened to him. One must admit the justice of Melville's belief that he was with Shakespeare and Dante: he did not claim to have equalled their art, only to have approximated their vision.

Thus the isolation of Melville was, at bottom, and in his maturity, neither the aristocrat's scorn of the mob, nor the snob's vanity, nor, most important of all, the rugged individualist's confident self-reliance. It derived, rather, from a consciousness of tragedy so acute and so deep-seated, that true kinship with any man but one who shared his tragic vision was a grotesque mockery. The spectator at *Oedipus Rex* who found that of all the audience he alone wept while the rest laughed, may be pardoned for having felt that between him and them there existed a gulf which he could never cross. No man has uttered more poignantly the desire for human brotherhood, and no man has watched with more profound bitterness as the inexorable pressure of the human facts destroyed the possibility of its fulfillment. How haunting, how insatiable was his wish to speak to another human being across the eternity of space which encompassed his

NOTES

NOTES

The pagination for all references to Melville's writings is that of *The Works*, Standard Edition, Constable, London, 1923.

1. *Pierre*, p. 195.
2. Julian Hawthorne, *Nathaniel Hawthorne and His Wife*, Boston, 1885, I, 407.
3. *Redburn*, p. 4.
4. *Moby Dick*, II, 103.
5. *Ibid.*, I, 144.
6. *Ibid.*, I, 144.
7. *Ibid.*, II, 101.
8. *Ibid.*, I, 144, 145.
9. "Hawthorne and His Mosses," in *Billy Budd and Other Prose Pieces*, pp. 132, 133.
10. One may observe the actual process of involution in the development of certain images through the novels. Beginning as external comparisons, these images acquire thought-content and deeper meanings, and often become symbols of the psychological problems which concern Melville. Interesting examples are: an Arctic explorer at the North Pole — *Mardi*, I, 135; *Pierre*, 231, 471; Cretan Labyrinth — *Moby Dick*, I, 31; II, 112; *Pierre*, 245; pyramid and mummy — *Moby Dick*, I, 4; II, 225; *Pierre*, 396–7; juggler — *Mardi*, I, 30; *Moby Dick*, I, 356; II, 110, 123; *Pierre*, 237, 253, 380; Laocoon — *Mardi*, II, 10; *Pierre*, 257.
11. *Hawthorne and His Wife*, I, 405–6.
12. My generalization is incomplete but true as it stands, and I make it only after the most

careful study of the matter. Compare notes 15, 18, 113.

13. *Pierre*, pp. 396–7.

14. *Moby Dick*, I, 133.

15. *Ibid.*, I, 349. The last sentence of this quotation, with its suggestion of the theme of inevitability or Fate which runs through *Moby Dick* and *Pierre*, recalls my statement that Fate meant for Melville the irresistible power which drove men deeper and deeper into themselves despite their most ardent desires to remain content with "the sweet felicities of ignorance." See notes 12, 18, 113.

For other examples of Melville's use of the image of sea and land in which Self and Universe coincide, see *Moby Dick*, I, 132–3; II, 329; *Pierre*, 396.

16. *Pierre*, p. 396.

17. *Hawthorne and His Wife*, I, 387.

18. These are further implications of "Fate" as Melville used the word. The relationship of Fate to the subconscious mind is an extremely interesting problem in *Pierre*.

19. *Moby Dick*, I, 230.

20. *Ibid.*, I, 253.

21. Meade Minnigerode, *Some Personal Letters of Herman Melville*, New York, 1922, p. 33.

22. *Moby Dick*, I, 132–3.

23. *Pierre*, p. 191.

24. *Ibid.*, pp. 471–2.

25. *Moby Dick*, II, 366.

26. *Pierre*, pp. 148, 150, 471, 500.

27. *Moby Dick*, I, 182.

28. *Ibid.*, I, 182–3.

29. *Ibid.*, I, 183.

30. *Hawthorne and His Wife*, I, 402.

31. *Ibid.*, I, 404.

32. Yeats, *Autobiographies*, New York, 1927, p. 234.

33. *Pierre*, p. 55.

34. *Ibid.*, pp. 55–6.

35. *Ibid.*, p. 56.

36. *Ibid.*, p. 57.

37. *Ibid.*, p. 70.

38. *Ibid.*, p. 70.

39. *Ibid.*, p. 90.

40. *Ibid.*, pp. 90–91. This speech is so clearly related in both thought and imagery to one of Ahab's most important speeches ("All visible objects, man, are but as pasteboard masks . . . strike through the mask! . . . " [*Moby Dick*, I, 204]), that it should be kept in mind when interpreting Ahab's words. The implications of the likeness unfortunately do not fall within the scope of this essay.

41. *Ibid.*, p. 123.

42. *Ibid.*, p. 124.

43. *Ibid.*, p. 126.

44. *Ibid.*, p. 126.

45. *Ibid.*, p. 127.

46. J. M. Murry, *Keats and Shakespeare*, Oxford, 1925, p. 121.

47. Keats, *Letters*, Oxford, 1935, p. 68.

48. *Keats and Shakespeare*, p. 135. Murry's remarks on Keats clarify in curious ways many problems in Melville. Though his devotion to Christ often outweighs his fidelity to Keats, his comments are unusually penetrating.

49. *Moby Dick*, II, 79–80.

50. *Ibid.*, II, 58–9.

51. *Ibid.*, II, 68.

52. *Pierre*, p. 290. He had already voiced his exasperation with Goethe in a letter to Hawthorne written while at work on *Moby Dick*. See *Hawthorne and His Wife*, I, 406.

53. *Pierre*, pp. 372, 409, 418, *et. al.*

54. *Ibid.*, p. 421.

55. *Ibid.*, p. 422. By the same token, he rejected the technique of the nineteenth-century novel because of its "false, inverted attempts at systematizing eternally unsystemizable elements." He was many years ahead of his time in recognizing the limitations of the too-simple motive-action-consequence formula of fiction: it is too often lost sight of that the unusual character of *Moby Dick* and *Pierre* derives partly from the fact that their creator was an artistic rebel, and not entirely from the fact that he was a unique phenomenon. See on this matter *Pierre*, pp. 198–9; also the pertinent implications of his contrast of "prose" with "poetry" in both art and life, on pp. 180 and 191.

56. *Ibid.*, p. 403.

57. *Moby Dick*, II, 181.

58. See Charles Olson's "Lear and Moby Dick," in *Twice A Year*, No. 1, 1938.

59. Caroline F. E. Spurgeon, *Shakespeare's Imagery*, New York, 1936, pp. 338–40.

60. *Moby Dick*, I, 152.

61. *Ibid.*, I, 252.

62. *Ibid.*, I, 252.

63. *Ibid.*, I, 211.

64. *Ibid.*, II, 327.

65. *Ibid.*, I, 229.

66. *Ibid.*, I, 209.

67. *Ibid.*, I, 209.

68. *Ibid.*, I, 230.

69. *Ibid.*, I, 230.

70. *Ibid.*, I, 232.

71. *Ibid.*, I, 154.

72. *Ibid.*, I, 328.

73. *Ibid.*, II, 253.

74. *Ibid.*, I, 211.

75. *Ibid.*, II, 282.

76. *Ibid.*, I, 253.

77. *Ibid.*, I, 153.

78. *Pierre*, p. 237.

79. *Moby Dick*, I, 209.

80. *Ibid.*, II, 284; I, 160; I, 253; II, 238.

81. *Ibid.*, II, 230. Since, in Melville's "theology," pagan terms were so often mingled with Christian concepts, and Christian terms with pagan concepts, this discussion necessarily makes use of figurative rather than literal language.

82. See, for example, the markings in his copy of Hawthorne's *Mosses* (now in Widener Library).

83. *Hawthorne and His Wife*, I, 387–8.

84. *Ibid.*, I, 404.

85. *Moby Dick*, II, 230.

86. *Ibid.*, II, 239.

87. *Ibid.*, II, 270.

88. *Ibid.*, II, 190.

89. *Ibid.*, II, 122.

90. "Thus, in the Enthusiast to Duty, the heaven-begotten Christ is born. . . ." *Pierre*, p. 149. For comments on the "influence" of Carlyle, see Robert S. Forsythe's Introduction to the *Americana Deserta* edition of *Pierre*, New York, 1930.

91. *Moby Dick*, II, 119.

92. For examples of recurrent imagery, see the mountain images on pp. 147, 252, 396, 424. On the Hamlet-analogy see Forsythe, *op. cit.* The Memnon Stone is on pp. 189–91.

93. *Pierre*, pp. 476–84.

94. *Ibid.*, p. 475.

95. *Ibid.*, p. 471.

96. *Ibid.*, p. 471.

97. *Ibid.*, p. 499.

98. *Ibid.*, p. 127.

99. *Ibid.*, p. 126.

100. *Ibid.*, p. 127.

101. *Ibid.*, p. 127.

102. *Moby Dick*, I, 133.

103. *Ibid.*, II, 182.

104. *Ibid.*, II, 181.

105. *Pierre*, p. 505.

106. *Moby Dick*, I, 229–30.

107. *Ibid.*, I, 253.

108. *Pierre*, p. 483.

109. *Moby Dick*, II, 366.

110. *Pierre*, p. 125. Solitude he believed to be the inevitable lot of every great mind. See p. 232.

111. *Moby Dick*, II, 341.

112. *Pierre*, p. 471.

113. *Moby Dick*, I, 212. Here again is the meaning of Fate suggested on p. 5.

114. *Moby Dick*, II, 190.

115. *Pierre*, p. 471.

BIBLIOGRAPHY

BIBLIOGRAPHY

The following list includes only books which have some bearing, no matter how remote, upon *Moby Dick* and *Pierre*. To my knowledge, no works exist upon the subject of this essay, though Charles Olson's "Lear and Moby Dick" is a necessary complement to it. I have learned far more about Melville from Keats, Shakespeare, the Jacobean drama, Yeats, and Joseph Conrad, than from any critical works on Melville himself; so that the list which follows is, in a sense, a mere formality.

Arvin, Newton, *Hawthorne*, Boston, 1929.

Braswell, William, *Herman Melville and Christianity*, University of Chicago Libraries, 1934.

Curl, Vega, *Pasteboard Masks: Fact as Spiritual Symbol in the Novels of Hawthorne and Melville*, Cambridge, Mass., 1931.

Damon, S. Foster, "Pierre the Ambiguous," *Hound and Horn*, Vol. II, No. 2 (1929), pp. 107–118.

Forsythe, Robert S., Introduction to *Pierre*, *Americana Deserta* series, New York, 1930.

Freeman, John, *Herman Melville*, London, 1926.

Hawthorne, Julian, *Nathaniel Hawthorne and His Wife*, Boston, 1885.

Hawthorne, Nathaniel, *The American Notebooks*, ed. Randall Stewart, New Haven, 1932.

Homans, George C., "The Dark Angel: The Tragedy of Herman Melville," *New England Quarterly*, Vol. V, No. 4 (1932), pp. 699–730.

BIBLIOGRAPHY

Lewisohn, Ludwig, *Expression in America*, New York, 1932.

Minnigerode, Meade, *Some Personal Letters of Herman Melville and a Bibliography*, New York, 1922.

Mumford, Lewis, *Herman Melville*, New York, 1929.

Murry, John Middleton, *Keats and Shakespeare*, Oxford, 1925.

Murry, John Middleton, *Studies in Keats*, Oxford, 1930.

Murry, John Middleton, "Metaphor," *Shakespeare Criticism, 1919–1935*, Oxford, 1936.

Olson, Charles, "Lear and Moby Dick," *Twice a Year*, No. 1, Fall–Winter, 1938, pp. 165–189.

Paltsits, Victor Hugo (editor), *Family Correspondence of Herman Melville*, New York Public Library Bulletin, Vol. 33, Nos. 7 and 8.

Spurgeon, Caroline F. E., *Shakespeare's Imagery*, New York, 1936.

Watson, E. L. Grant, "Melville's *Pierre*," *New England Quarterly*, Vol. III, No. 2 (1930).

Weaver, Raymond B., *Herman Melville, Mariner and Mystic*, New York, 1921.

Weaver, Raymond B. (editor), Introduction to *Journal Up the Straits*, New York, 1935.